Thira

Thira

poems

Susan Roney-O'Brien

Cover design by Shay Culligan

Cover art: Mural at Knossos, Crete

ISBN: 978-1-950462-96-4

Kelsay Books Inc.

kelsaybooks.com

502 S 1040 E, A119
American Fork, Utah 84003

For Curt, the wise and trusted, and Pat of the great heart

Thira, a Cycladic island in the Mediterranean, now called Santorini, was the site of a volcanic eruption that sent a tidal wave into Crete, sixty miles to the south, and darkened the skies with ash, changing the weather in the region. The island had served as a Minoan outpost, and in 1967, when archaeologists uncovered the ruins of the Minoan city of Akrotiri preserved under fifteen feet of ash, they discovered clay pipes providing hot and cold water, flush toilets, astonishing frescos, and no human remains. Because of the circular structure of the island, the obvious prosperity of the people, and the fine deep harbor, some scholars entertain the thought that Thira was Atlantis.

"Museums would be dead places indeed
if we did not imagine the cup in a living hand."
J. Lesley Fitton

Acknowledgments

Echo & Spark: "At harvest," "Embark," "Hive," "Stars and bones," "Sojourners," "Watching"

Mediterranean Poetry: "Caress," "Evocation," "Fresco," "In Yellow Light," "Olive Tree," "Waking from love," "Watching"

Copperfield Review: "The Minoans Speak"

Contents

What Light Is Borne from the Center of the Earth

Hornet Nest

Spit-built layers—a gray bomb—hangs
from the hundred-year-old lilac
that drapes the barway,
a lantern full of hum and dark,
and when our son wields a rake,
breaks the nest, hornets erupt.
The cradle of larvae falls.
Some wasps attack his eyes
while others fly into the mouth
of the ruined hive that
collapses into itself,
sides rising like islands
rimming the caldera
hollowed by its fall.

When Strong Enough and Beautiful

Olive Tree

The womb of the moon is the olive tree,
leaves enfold its slender slip.
Moon glides among limbs and
still blind, feels its way
out of darkness.

At harvest

when earth eases our hungers, we reach
into dry stream's channel,
find seams that line the bed
and unearth clay.

Our fingers pluck out soil and roots,
bones of fishes, stones, then pack
gleaned, clean clay tight and carry it back
to spread on white linen in the sun.

We wait then pound dried grit,
sift it through nets, gather the dust,
moisten with caught rain, drain and wrap
for the artists, the women who make,

who coil-build clay, shape amphorae
for oil, water and grain, rhytons for wine
and small closed jars etched with birds
for saffron.

When, in good time, all pots are formed
and sun-dried, we call our village to us,
light brushwood in the pit we hollowed,
and on charcoal and ash, stack pots

upside down, layer upon layer,
shield with shards to keep them from wind
then lay more brush on top
and light the flame.

All day and into night, we tend and talk.
At dawn, we lift vessels from ash,
a kind of birth, a leaving of the nest
when strong enough and beautiful.

What the Waves Said

Listen, each smoothed stone, every
shell I carry is a story I tell.
My voice has no beginning,
tide no end.

A drowned river pulls prows,
eye-marked, toward deep and blue
and dark. Wind bellies out
square sails bedecked
with dolphins. My salt licks resin
from hulls. Far from land,

gulls abandon all ships. I roll
great pithoi. Olive oil sloshes
inside. Trade's abacus
clicks in anticipation. My sea roads
lead from Cyprus copper to tin
men forge into bronze.

But I am Mediterranean. I am sea.
I take ships. Etesian winds,
Meltemi build waves high.
Minoan traders die.

Octopodes

Pulling limbs behind,
they ride the current, ambling yet
                    driven.
We watch them flow
beneath outcroppings and into caves,
change color and texture to hide their place
then spear them,
                    turn them inside out,
roll bodies between stones
hang them in sun to dry,
and lay them above fire for roasting:
salt and flesh and sea.

Jewel

From Egypt's valley, gold,
its unearthing, worth
told to our merchants who
enjoined those most trusted

to choose one moldmaker
who incises honeybee body
into stone, pours molten gold
to fill the hollow.

Cooled, removed, the cone
of beebody smoothed,
beaten wings unfurl
on the breast of our priestess.

Fresco

For beauty,
cordon the surface off,
stretch taut string
onto lime plaster skim.
On damp fullness, inscribe
sinopia lion, antelope, lily.

Let Mother define
your palette—
lapis, malachite, bistre,
giallorino, and ochre.
Pulverize scoria,
let bone white grant
open space, rest.

Dip brush in pigment
mixed with rain.
Let tint seep in
like sunrise dyes cloud,
or the scent of grapes
steeps in still air

and when your hand
tires, and light fades,
put the tools
of your craft away.

Know roar, leap, blossom.

To start grapes for wine

dig deep; comb fine the sandy soil,
combine dried eelgrass, potash, dung
in the hole, then on a lost moon night
when stars alone cast light into sea,
plant the mother root.

Cover as you would
a child who fears the dark, knowing
roots in dark will branch and swell,
spread and anchor against wind,
against the deep reach of parch
before rains fall.

When tendrils unfurl, cut away
all but two; cut back long shoots.
Reduce vine length to half.
Trim again to foster heavy canes.
First year, expect little. Keep plants
clean, cultivate around roots.

Come winter, prune and weave.
When grapes begin, swell
along curved canes, rest
sheltered from gust and blow
safe from bottom rot, they will ripen
in bowls of their own growing.

Weaving

In wooden arms of olive the sun nests,
throws branched shadows against earth.

When Saffron Mother, Mistress of Wild Bees
lets weavers begin,

we interlace weft, walk among hanging warp
and dangling disks of clacking clay.

How like sparrows' work, this day-by-day
building of cloth from beaten flax.

Saffron

We ascend the slope where
plantings seem a purple shadow—
where crocus upon crocus
raises slender leaves
from nests of dried grasses,
opens, and we gather
low-growing blossoms,
these yellow throats, these
thrice-blessed gifts
in plaited baskets, carry them
down from the mountain.

Sun reaches out from sea,
casts fronds of lavender,
bronze and rose into waiting dawn
and we sit in circles of seven,
release red-gold strands,
stigmas of the flowers—
three filaments that can be nothing
but saffron.

Keepers

When among
our island village one
breathes out and there is no in,
we, the keepers, begin: sea-cleanse our bodies,
scour hollows with deep song, and what rises lifts words
beyond themselves, beyond
definition and history,
becomes shudder
beneath wings,
violet sky,
thunder,
silence.

Once
our bodies
stand purified,
we smooth eyelids
of death's blind eyes,
remove life's garments,
and sponge duty, dust away.
Then, when time tempers flesh, and flesh turns
stone, we pray, await pliancy's slow
return, speak of days without,
days of empty hands,
scalding star nights,
cold moon.

Throughout
our lamentations,
the body waits beyond
grief and fear, hears nothing,
feels nothing. Finally we split the ribs,
open the chest, lift out the heart,
wrap it in cloth, wash
its emptied nest
in wine.
Using fine
saffron-dyed thread,
we bind slit flesh, oil cold skin,
wind linen between and around each limb,
and anoint with honey, consign
the body to death, having
held life within.

When Mother

calls her warrior
we bear him on our shoulders
to our people's tomb above the sea.

We lay him, head toward sunrise,
feet toward night
on wave-pebbled chamber floor

and at his side align his dagger
twisted upon his death as sacrifice.
The old priestess seals the door.

Outside the tomb we gather,
dance him safe,
set him free

with flutes of bone,
bronze-tongued bells, song,
dance him home.

The dead with us

              sip long Her gifts—
this is the cheek an aunt stroked, this palm,
the way the hand lifts in greeting or alarm
is a father's long gone from this life
into the arms of the Mother who grants
time, a gift She knows, honors
and understands.

She weaves sloughed skins of snakes
while the living drape her shoulders
encircle her breasts. They are prayer
as birth begins, their sleep teaches
when bodies cannot persist.

In cold they lie, icons of hiss and writhe,
and when sun rises warm, slip skins,
become strong, lithe, young,
and this is the promise death holds:
memory, shape-echo.

Cast skins speak as sun comes. Listen.
Cliffs ring with birdsong.
Hollow-boned bodies lift into wind.
Death is the lightening, the flick of spirit,
the kiss of the Mother.

Rain on the Mountain

Steam sheathes;
drops release, hiss,
and from this distance
Mother's fiery heart
shrouds its heat,
parting us from Her.
We children of thunder,
exist only
        within
each others' armspans.
It is a gift of the Mother,
this dimming of fire,
this opacity.
        Even in disunion,
when faith's abyss howls
hollow-eyed, laid bare,

She is always here.

Stars and bones

foretold their coming
and when Minoan ships anchored
beyond stone cliffs, we of the island
rejoiced. The sea eased their entry
and we opened our homes, led them
through olive groves to crocus beds
below peregrine nests high on the mountain,
and they sowed our land, accepted
our priestess as their own, honored bee
and dolphin, fished blue sea, built with us
until all we children of the Mother
wove our lives together; simple nets
cast from earth into tide.

The Minoans Speak

We left that land
                when ground shook
despite our prayers. We lined
          baskets of bread and grain,
jugs of oil, wheat sheaves
                        on the stepped east altar,
set out small clay figures, arms raised
to assure good crops, rain.
                         When still soil rose like dust,
we came to the peak, bore lambs for sacrifice.

When lambs did not appease,
we slaughtered a sacred bull
presented it to the goddess,
sure the wine of such blood,
flowing below frescoes
                    through furrows
                            and into bronze vessels
would placate wrath.

                But when no offering sufficed,
when roadbeds cracked, when
foundations of our homes heaved, collapsed,
                we called upon the priest to intercede
and in the chamber between west and east,
a ring of silver and iron
                on his sinistral hand,
pitiless out of fear, he
                plunged a dagger
into a young warrior's throat
then
        laid a boar's head lance across
the stilled chest.

The altar shuddered.

                                        Amphorae shattered.

West of the village,

                    when earth shook

bones of the dead

                exploded against tomb walls.

From Crete Minoans Come

When the map emerges—mountain, sea,
our island defined by a broken line,
they find safe harbor beneath the peak
that breathes smoke,
a cleft split red where rivers underlie
earth's mantle, where magma roars,
spits blood of old fires.

Roots

Progeny of night and earth and olive tree,
we silver leaves, we moon-drawn
transitory children
pluck dark fruit, press for light
and all the while
olive roots hold earth in place
within rolling time,
gathered space.

Atana

Gathering

In lavender shade of olive trees,
our priestess speaks of roots' soil journey,
a reach and hold that none can see.

She tells a dream of life's end,
how she will be set free of breath,
that like grass or olive leaves, she

will have no use for words, for memory,
death easing all senses, and she
will need nothing but air and rain

and earth, the caress of light, wind,
deep roots pushing through soil,
no knowing, neither pain nor joy.

We of the village listen and watch
her frail hands, birds taking wing,
and try to understand. I begin to sing.

Smiling, the old woman brushes my palm,
adds breath to song; entwining voices
climb toward sun.

One

No mother like the sea, yet sea
is She who is Mother, who encompasses
sand, pebbles, scales, drowned ships
loaded with dreams, who glitters
in moonlight while waves
heave stones worn smooth
onto land.

All gifts are Hers to give us
although Her hands are briny
and Her winds blow sand into our eyes,
for She is wind as well that drives our ships
to Egypt.

And when I pick a crocus from Her mountain,
watch planters bend and dig and stand,
or pat soil around an iris,
Mother is the earth cupped
in my hands.

On the lip of the Aegean, I stand within
Mother's voice. The wind catches
a strand of sea grass, blows my cloak
sail-full. All about me, gulls praise,
spume anoints my feet.
The sun dips its fire
into sea.

Atana and the Priestess

Each time we come together,
we embrace.
           In between us
and alone after,
the blossoming.

Atana Asks

Does the octopus taste my skin,
know blood rivers within my body?
How does the honeybee pray?

Are waves and clouds hymns
wind plays on sea, on sky? Who listens?
Who understands such harmony?

When I raise my arms in praise,
does Mother see me? Must prayer
be learned or can each breath become paean?

Does the bee thank the Mother
for a crocus blossoming? Is honey
the prayer of the bee?

What does the octopus teach me of spirals?
Will I learn to pray open-eyed when
I cast aside blood beneath skin?

Bull Dance

Joyful
I hone my body,
seek discipline
to honor the Mother
whose fierce, all-seeing eye
is sea where sun falls,
earth where calves bleat
and cry,
      and from which I,
Atana, the light dancer,
           scent on wind,
fly
   onto horned crescent moon,
lift my body,
        flip high and grip hide
with open fingers, thrust
legs to sky and
arch off,
         my prayer, my invocation,
fluid as a dolphin's glide.

At the Red Beach

That pearl moon night
the red cliffs shifted. I clambered
down. Stones broke loose beneath,
cascaded ahead as though eager
to roll deep into water. The dye maker,
wrapped in soot-stained cloth,
tended her pot. *Atana?*

I nodded. *Lonely work that,*
only wave voices. She fed the blaze,
stirred. *Enough for me.*

Flame light painted steam.
From under the sea that is sky
a few pale stars gleamed
while murex shells climbed, then
dropped deep: small lives
sacrificed for beauty
if any life is small.

I shall never wear garments
of rich purple, the dye maker
laughed. *But you will.*

Steam and smoke rose, intermingled
like dreams that colored day. *I've seen*
the priestess' eyes follow you.
When you rise to priestess I
will dye the cloth, weave your robe.
Now I boil shelled sea beasts
that live to give their lives.

I turned, climbed red cliffs,
watched full moon glide
in and out of clouds.

Eclipse

My sister spoke
of when the sun went dark—
some animal,
through blue and cloud
flew open-jawed;
the cavern of its mouth
cut sunlight black,
strung beads of spit
where it began.

She said it ate the sun
and all the land
was doused in night.

She wept
but old ones sang
of dawn, return of light,
and song overspread
darkness. Soon
chants, flutes and gongs
forced night from day
and the beast,
repulsed by revelry,
released its prey.

Watching

Oh, but there is good in this—
sun lifts at earth's edge
as night sinks roots
beneath olive trunks, and sky
swathes the blanched shell moon
in light, takes on day.

He rises from long shadow,
shades dark eyes, casts
weighted net into waves,
into light, openwork
falling through sky and sea.
Woven lines, sinking deep,

honeycomb sand, lie against
spent diatom's glimmer,
shroud seagrass. Between
net and surface, red mullet,
dusky perch, blennies glide,
until cinched, the sides

pull tight and he hauls the catch,
shimmering, onto land.
By high sun, he links
silver gills, wide mouths,
and hefts fish, ready for market,
to his side.

In Yellow Light

Flung along the shore after storm,
an octopus like a leaf lay,
a soft-bodied shadow—arms spread—
a waste of life and food and beauty.

I paint the sea that begins in me
onto amphorae, onto beaked jars,
capture color and line, green weed water
floods buff sides,

eight flowing arms like vines
reach and twine upon the surface,
overspreading. Octopus
rises, swims again.

Evocation

Yes, I remember.
His hand brushed my arm
in passing,
and after,
I sought signs—heat
a reddening—
but there were none.

Inside my body, sunlight began
and each time I saw him
in a grove of olives
or walking into the sea,
would will him to me,
invoke the Mother's
great embrace, summon
trees, waves, grasses
to bring him close

and when he came,
I feigned innocence, cast
my eyes down, strode
toward the marketplace
until he caught my hand
and I, done with play,
matched his gaze,
unwavering.

Waking from love

sea calls
         to sea
and out of dream

we fall
     into dark,
walk wave's wake,
awaken
         luminescence—
heartbeats of light
            ignite
stars
      beneath our feet
and we dance
where water and earth
become
        another,
a place without name,
the long breath
           between sea and land,
dark and dawn
        then
Mother's salt-green water
holds out
        strong arms, and we
float among stars.

Sea Change

After his brother's ship
heaved into port from Crete,
we three ate olives and cheese,
drank wine, shared fish fresh caught—
sweet harvest of earth and sea—
while I marked similarities:
strong, wide hands,
eyes blacker than sky,
movement beneath skin,
a kind of shimmering, like heat
in a rain-trance of drying

and the brother talked of family,
shipbuilders who felled cypress trees
to make the ship. The sea was calm,
he said, on the voyage.
The woolen sail held strong,
its deck-strung ropes allowed
the vessel to face headwinds.
The ropes, though,
needed a surer hand than his own,
and I knew my lover
would go from me.

                *

In darkness he and I
spoke of this—
his promise so late in the season,
but within time, he said, the ship
would carry him home
with riches from amphorae of oil
loaded into the hold.

In two days, first light,
the ship would sail.
I placed his hand upon my belly.
You must stay safe. We have a child
within, I told him, and
he called me *"my island, "*
and *Thira* displaced Atana as my name,

She who is home, said he, *untamed,*
my chosen. Then he lifted me from bed
and we woke his brother.

No better time, his brother said,
than when life begins
to secure your place, set sail
among seamen and merchants
and traders.

The men embraced.

       *

Harsh day; sun cuts
sharp shadows across sand. Gulls
drop mollusks onto rocks, roofs.
Already, the men are gone
to mind the loading.

I rub scented oil
onto my breasts and belly, dress
as though the Mother had said
today will mark the rest of my days

and walk through the town
determined. My sister joins me.
I tell her first
of tomorrow's journey,
then of the child beginning.
She cradles my hand
all the way to the harbor.

＊

Amphorae line the route
or ride strong shoulders
of rowers and seamen
to the ship—pots I built and glazed,
pots rich with oil
from my family's olive trees,
fruit we had plucked and pressed.
I remember the stone's turning,
the men yoked and straining.
My work holds our promise.

When the amphora
etched with my octopus passes,
I ask the youth to pause.
Reaching into my wrap I clasp
the gold sealing stamp—
a bee in a blossom,
my sign—drop it into the oil,
re-seal the stop.

What the Old Priestess Saw

From where she crouches
she can watch the mountain clear
of mist, swell at its base. The trembling.
Wisps of smoke. She draws threads
to line the basket—soft the spun flax,
sweet the dust of yellow crocus—
and vines wind along the hollow
like wind lifting, making basins in sand,
scooping shallow nests sun will find
and ocean water fill and smooth,
but she does not think of hollows,
she too is mountain.
The child stretches
in her womb.

No peregrines
slip through clouds to perch
on the cliff and sit through shudder.
Instead they ride valley breath, sea
exhalations spiral above mountain splits,
the vents from which steam escapes,
and sliding rocks foretell what she has felt
all along. Having seen what she has seen
she picks her words by weight,
lifts each like an infant to the sun,
speaks to save her child, herself,
all: *Woman of fire,*
stone and sky
has begun.

Cleft

When you left our island,
earth disgorged stone rivers.

A black and burning tide
encrusted the cliff side,

hissed steam as it spilled
into blue Aegean.

When sun climbed
and tide pulled back,

what had been molten
lay shattered;

black sand shrouded
the mountain.

Alone

I try to send each flutter, each
kick of our child within
to my lover, my trader,
try to catch him,
to reel him home to me,
to our island, but always see
only the ship that took him
and hear his brother's pride
as he described the building,
how cousins and fathers,
brothers and sons
stripped branches and bark,
hollowed what would be keel,
and used heat and steam
to shape the stern.

My lover's eyes filled
as his brother spoke and I wondered,
did he miss that life he'd turned from
when he settled here?

Seventeen men, his brother said,
slid and pushed the ship
into the sea
so water would swell wood,
create a seal before they added
board after board
to build up the keel, then finished
decks and rowing benches.
He described stretching linen
to cover the hull,

said how painstakingly
the family had painted
dolphins, waves and eyes,
finally seabirds
to give praise and thanks
to the Mother.

Three full moons have come and gone.
I see the ship in my mind,
but cannot see the father of my child.
Each morning,
the ocean yawns cold, empty;
its waves relentless, scrabble up
on shore, leave broken shells,
smoothed stones
when tide pulls back.

Storm

Wind whirls in from the west,
cyclone spins sea swirl, tumult.
And this day when I walk to the harbor
seeking his family ship,
gulls, their heads tucked in,
perch on boats pulled onto sand.

Last night, I felt my lover's weight
and even awake, I held his warmth
along my back, across my shoulders.
A dream, of course, but solid and yielding—
a kind of fruition I wanted most to feel.
And he was with me, here. I woke
sure of it. I woke placid,
fulfilled, at peace

but now sea and sky are warring.
Wind churns waves, pushes me
against beached ships, dislodges
the dream and I shudder from cold
where both he and the dream left me.

What Light Is Borne from the Center of the Earth

Portent

Clouds boil high
inside the alabastron of sky
when lightning strikes the olive tree,
shakes me from sleep, and by the time we reach the grove
flames tick like rain, dance dry wind,
leap from bough to bough trailing charred shadows.
                    We beat the flames.
Fire climbs from duff to topmost branches.
Smoke curdles air.

When dawn comes, the ground lies heavy
with downed limbs: scattered fardage
from a drowned ship.

No square sail flares in the harbor.

In Akrotiri

Shell heaps punctuate the shoreline
where our dye maker lies
who would sleep even beneath rags
if she could sleep, rags and moonlight.
She weeps. Sand shifts. Grit encrusts
thin lips, trickles from her hair. She spits,
pulls herself up, lifts driftwood from wrack,
fits it into the fire. Flames flicker against wind.
Her song plaits night and tide. Shells
clatter across shingle, a gull cries.

My beloved, when breath died,
I could not close your eyes until
light came, until sunrise.
I would have died beside you
if not for our child's cry.

She sings as nimbus swells from sea,
light swathes her body as though
sun is soon to rise, but rain hisses,
spatters the coast, large drops
darken mollusk shells, pebbles
that shudder—hills built on sand.
She stirs the vat. Clots of murex snails,
spiral-coiled, boil, bubble up, surrender
to heat, sink and slip beneath,
bequeath the distillate of purple dye.

Mother's Child

They come at first light, the women,
all speaking at once,
some wrapped in fine wool,
others bearing loomed cloth, gifts—
pots of white beans, olives.
The midwife ties a sloughed snakeskin
just below my knee—to honor
Ilithyia, to remind
that life is change, a tide. She says
I am serpent waking from cold,
new life grows from within split skin.

She mixes dittany in wine. I take
the mixture into my mouth.
It will ease the pain, she says,
then another rolls my gown
above my hips. The midwife
bends into my body, fingertips
dripping oil between spread legs,
and kneads the opening,
now the size of an egg, she tells me.

The child within is dolphin, whale.
No matter. The moon pulls all
and I am sea and sand, rush and drag.
Someone takes my hand, breathes slow,
tells me to follow her breath
so I will be carried, so my child
will emerge whole and strong—
all flesh and cry into this life—

and when I feel the body
solid and slick find the passage,
I cry out and my sisters brace
my back against their own. I push
and press my body down while
the midwife holds palms hard against
my belly, massages life toward air.
One woman begins to sing.
Another, laughing, says the head
crowns, *oh—dark curls, shoulders,*
arms, legs, toes.

The midwife lifts my son so I may see.
He shivers in the air, wails,
and one wraps him in linen,
brings him to my breast. I cradle
his small body upon my own—his
homeland, and I am floating
into the Mother's sleep,
the country he comes from,
the place he knows
and can return to now
only in dream.

The Priestess Addresses the Village

There is time for all things and all things take time.
Upon my longed-for death, when the Mother takes me,
another will begin. Even now, she rises among you,
a lily opening upon the Mother's breast.
Within her, belief is gold.

Do not weep. I am old;
my bones resist change, wind
blows within. My skin unfolds,
loosens from its moorings, my eyes
dim to focus inward
where wide time runs
through all who abide
within the Mother.

You ask how you will know her, this new voice
who doesn't know herself she is chosen.
You will know by her strength. She will come
with dreams, new life, a way
to thwart cataclysm. She will guide

with simple words. Take heed.
The Mother is within her
and she within the Mother.
Listen and follow. Leave
fear and doubt for the sea to take.
You will know her
through her prescience, her wisdom.
Her eyes are Mother's;
her counsel, mine.

Griffin

I dream a griffin, eagle-winged,
her great curved beak clamped tight,
held from flesh.
Lion flanks, thighs rest at the ready
against a lily-etched throne
where light laves the priestess,
her gold bee necklace
suspended between breasts.

The griffin tilts her head,
eyes hone in on me,
the watcher in the dream.
I raise my arm to stroke her,
to let her know I follow the Mother
but she lifts herself from rest
into a spread-wing crouch.
Her eyes gleam fire and blood.

Horned beak cracks, opens.
I cry out. The old priestess
slides to the floor.
Beads and bees unstring.

All daughters, mothers now

                              prevail
through light and dark, nights
and days,
              blaze up
beneath the budding moon,
the moon when all things waken.
Infants cry
                    and we are tide.
      Milk
thrums through breasts
as memory throws us
back
        into desire, reflects
from the sounding board of want
and we come
                    to lips and tongue,
                                  come
to moon pull, rounded pebbles
drummed by the draw of current,
beyond our control.
      Need
is the moon
that shapes our time.

Caress

The hand of love is upon my son
whose father vanished in water and wind.

Full moon tidefall pulls black sand back,
strews kelp along flats

where he pulled in fish, where I fill
spaces between what he and I had planned

and what has come to be—story and song
instead of his strong hand leading

our son into manhood. Oh for one caress
of his palm against my cheek.

My child, your hunger

rises, night birds' orison, and I open my eyes, cradle
you in my arms and take the steep path
waveside to nurse you by Mother's sea.

Again your cry stopped the dream—
flames like molten wings streak black sky,
fiery streams raze the village,

shroud seacoast in steam, then ash,
feathers from a plague of crows
heap upon white stones.

The ocean rises; its cold seabed swallows
hills, cliffs, homes, crests and pulls
rubble and muck, holds it, washes it out and back

and Mother's voice like a heartbeat begins,
tolls inside my body: *Take your place.*
I say your name. You hold the time to come.

Then waves wash past the village. I stand
purple-robed, alone before our people. My son,
each night when dream returns, ash fills my throat.

The Dye Maker Seeks to Know

You say the Mother gives
what we need, that She teaches
through love. But if She is as you say,
why does She shatter our walls, allow
earth to smash amphorae, crack frescoes
so that even you fear?

You say the Mother takes
our lives into Her own body—
what wounds us hurts Her; but our hearts
are fish dying on a line. Why
does She shun our sacrifices,
our holy flames?

You say prayer and song
will reach Her ears, will show us
the way, and we have sung, we have
prayed until our lips are raw
with wanting, our voices
hoarse and frayed.

You say the Mother will save us.
Why is the sun caught
in a net of ash above liquid fire,
tumbling stone? Why must
I carry my only child,
leave our home?

The Plea

How can I be believed, one woman alone
in the dark of doubt and denial?
No one wants to think we must leave
our lives behind, not the dye maker,
that most sea-wise sister, not the village:
fishers, traders, farmers and friends.

I speak of signs: vents exhaling smoke
from the mountain, lizards scurrying north,
swarms of bees. Mother's earth rears up
like an antelope captured and brought
to a hostile land. Dolphins, octopuses
wash onto shore. Earth cracks. Fissures

expand. I bend to place my strongest hand
within a crevice open at my feet. Sand
flows like water but earth does not mend.
I pray Mother will help me find the way
to save our people, pray that their belief
extends to me, Her vessel,

that they will understand, flee.

First of Last Days

Past days wheel in light. Night resounds with voices.
The moon, wave-drowned, slides beneath lined cliffs—
layered when earth flowed out of mountain throat
and fire burnished land. Now, where we stand shifts. Wind
twists from the south. The mountain swells.

Know me now. I am eyes, lips, tongue. I am the promise
Mother keeps, She who would send us away
before earth surges, writhes beneath our soles,
sweeps us into runnels of fire, and ash smothers us,
before ocean swallows land.

Voice Without

Our Mother's skies
breathe dust and cloud.
Her mountains quake,
earth slides where once
crocus bloomed.

We are not inside Her
but She in us
and we comprise bone and blood,
muscle, nerve and skin
of her body.

We are Her song,
we, Her ears and eyes,
we, Her hands held out
to comfort, to caress.
How could I
not have known?

We hold Her life in our hands.
We must carry
our children,
our art and joy,
the beauty She gives,
the lessons of hive and nest

to keep Her alive. We must
begin again, all of us,
one breath.

Prophesy

When the shudders begin,
my heart quakes. Outside heart's hive,
trees' utmost branches quiver;

mountain fissures breathe steam
while peregrines widen slow circles
over water's deep blue pulse.

Earth whispers the secret
in Mother's voice, through dream.
Ash-swarm lifts ebony wings,

molten stone hisses down slopes,
over cliffs, into the sea. Steam.

I am fish, the ocean boiling.
I am lava, once stone.
I am sea, waves roiling.

Ash rains fall onto Akrotiri, bury
streets, sift into hallways, smother

rooms, drift onto pithos,
over looms half-strung, lutes, drums.
Cinders silence Mother's voice, blacken

Her children's hands, stop our throats.
Dreams show what will come
and clear a way: vessels,

loaded with our people, our stores.
Oh, Mother, open our eyes.
Help us believe.

Duties

Hordes of ants transport eggs away
on black backs. Honeybees, wasps
collect, swarm, escort their queens
far from the mountain.
Swallows fall from the sky,
lie against rubble and schist.
Even dolphins, cuttlefish
wash up on tides
when no tides exist.

I say what you must know,
but will not admit—
these days thick with omens,
full of dark—open a new time.
Gather those you love.
If you are the Mother's child,
know She watches. If not, persist;
Her gifts encompass even
your disbelief, and are limitless.

Hive

We who flee before eruption scuttle through chambers,
gather saffron, thyme, barley, rye, dried fish, wine
for the journey, fill our needs to begin new lives:

honey on the comb, sheep and goats, oil-filled amphorae,
seeds and roots, grape vines, and our brushes, pots,
hoes and nets, looms, wheels, cups, knives, hides, blankets.

We gather what we need to survive as does an old queen bee
when she dances the young to birth a hive outside
a new queen's realm. They swarm air as blue as sea, as wide.

We leave what we cannot carry, name or sing—
moon's smoking fingers through boughs, children's first steps,
first words, the last caress of the gone,

paths of spring's bee flight among purple crocuses high
upon the mountain. I take my son's hand.

Embark

In the corridor of smooth stones, faces
all turn toward sea.

        We rattle dreams' cage,
lean against each other

           sing the note
made when waves meet shore.

Between lives
        we wait in this passage—

all signs aligned: stars caught
in sky's black wings.

Sojourners

The trapped blaze draws us
back to where it began—
        fire inundates arteries
from the heart of the earth,
and latent memories spill,
        sweet carillon of a country
we want to believe in.

We want
to have come from there
where we lost and now
unearth our people, in a cadence
                we carry forward in our bodies.

Some of us know what was found,
           ocean-shaped stones, shells that sing
from the hands of women,
           a new map to our lost land
that compasses neither Cancer nor Capricorn—
but heat, red heat, molten light

and runes   old script in an unknown language.
We highlight gone with broken lines.

We do not label, do not name, but
we who seek find our way.

Cradle and All

Black lava, red spatter, metamorphic schists—
the plate-stacked strata of Santorini cliffs
mark time laid down—

all fire and hiss—with each eruption.
Before Santorini collapsed.
Minoans paved streets,

painted frescoes; young women lifted full
rhytons of wine; men cast bronze-
tipped tools, raised blades near Akrotiri,

each extraordinary life more treasured than
saffron. Now on the sand-swathed caldera coast,
from beneath the pumice mantle,

diggers, haulers, the brushers and sifters,
unearth walls of homes, red slip pots, but
no bones, no teeth, no human remains

lodged in layers of loss. Before swarms of ash
descended, before lava flowed,
before the mountain itself

exploded, and earthquakes shuddered
through houses, rocking stone off falling stone,
where did they go?

Bibliography

Clark, John O.E. and Stiegeler, Stella. **The Facts on File Dictionary of Earth Science.** New York: Checkmark Books, 2000.

Cline, Eric H., editor. **The Oxford Handbook of the Bronze Age Aegean.** New York: Oxford University Press, 2010.

Fitton, J. Lesley. **Minoans**. London: The British Museum Press, 2002.

Groenewegen-Frankfort, H.A. **Arrest and Movement: Space and Time in the Art of the Ancient Near East.** London: The Belknap Press of Harvard University Press, 1987.

Preziosi, Donald and Hitchcock, Louise A. **Aegean Art and Architecture.** New York: Oxford University Press, 1999.

From the Land of the Labyrinth: Minoan Crete, 3000-1100 BC. New York: Alexander S. Onassis Public Benefit Foundation, 2008.

Notes

Almost every poem in this manuscript has been improved musically and literally through the sensitive ruthlessness of Curt Curtin, my most trusted and respected reader.

Thank you, Eleanor Wilner for your care and my extraordinary family for their patience: Philip, Caitlin, Jeffrey, Kevin, Lauren, Benjamin, Jacob, Madeline and William.

In addition, I have also been blessed with others who have enlarged my perceptions, sharpened my narrative skills and opened lyric possibilities: Patty Youngblood, Clair Degutis, Mary Jo Moore, Pam Bernard, Patricia Fargnoli, Linda Warren, Dan Lewis, Eve Rifkah, R. Joyce Heon, Michael Milligan, Dorothy Anderson, Peter Radley, Susan Sedgwick, Rhett Watts, Lisa Barthelson, Dorothy Magadieu, and Carolyn Crane.

I thank dear friends who have supported me, whose understanding and love of both word and image have kept me honest and kept me writing: Anita Cook, Therese Goulet, Terry Farish and Lori Rabeler.

Thank you, Rhys Townsend, for providing research and support.

Two poems, "From Crete Minoans Come" and "Sojourners", were inspired by a Carolyn Crane Collaged Map that she created using various papers and white Conte crayon—winter, 2011.

"The Minoans Speak" is based on a section of J. Lesley Fitton's fine book, **Minoans**. The documentation and description of human sacrifice at Cretan/Minoan hands both challenged my thinking and enabled me to let go of the narrow path I had been writing about in the poems.

"Keepers" originally lacked the reference to honey as a type of preservation. At a "First Monday" poetry reading in Worcester, MA, Janet Guerrin mentioned the practice. I found the reference accurate and changed the poem to reflect the new material.

"In Yellow Light" and the definition of the main character as a potter came from studying illustrations of Minoan pottery in **From the Land of the Labyrinth: Minoan Crete, 3000-1700 B.C.** a catalogue issued in conjunction with the exhibition held at the Onassis Cultural Center, New York, March 13-September 13, 2008.

About the Author

Susan Roney-O'Brien has published *Bone Circle* (Kelsay Books, 2018), (*Legacy of the Last World* (Word Poetry, 2016) and two chapbooks, *Earth* (Cat Rock Publications, 2011) and *Farmwife* (Nightshade Press, 2000). Her work has been nominated for several Pushcart Prizes. She is a member of the 4X4 Poet and Artist Collaborative. Susan works with international students and local writers, curates a monthly poetry venue, is a board member of the Worcester County Poetry Association, and is the summer writing series coordinator for the Stanley Kunitz Boyhood Home in Worcester, Massachusetts. Her work has been translated into Braille and Mandarin. She lives In Massachusetts with photographer Philip O'Brien.

Kelsay Books

Made in the USA
Middletown, DE
08 December 2020

26948275R00054